I LOVE THIS LITTLE GIRL WHO ENTERED THE WORLD WITH A BANG.

AS I EMBRACE YOU, MY HEART FILLS WITH JOY AND GRATITUDE, BRINGING A SMILE TO MY FACE.

AND AS I LOOK INTO YOUR EYES, I FEEL THIS SPECIAL CONNECTION I NEVER FELT BEFORE.

YOU ARE MY DREAM COME TRUE..

I MARVEL AT HOW SPECIAL
YOU ARE

YOUR GIGGLES, SMILES, AND HUGS MAKE ME LOVE YOU EVEN MORE.

EVER SINCE YOU ARRIVED, A RADIANT TRANSFORMATION HAS TOUCHED EVERY ASPECT OF MY LIFE.

YOUR RADIANCE ILLUMINATES THE ROOM, CAPTIVATING EVERYONE IN YOUR PRESENCE.

I LOVE THIS LITTLE GIRL.
HER HAIR WAS SO FLUFFY,
LIKE A CLOUD CASCADING
DOWN, AS SHE SKIPPED BY.

I LOVE THIS LITTLE GIRL. HER CHEEK, A SUBTLE HINT OF PINK, GRACING HER FACE, AND IN HER SWEET EMBRACE, MY SPIRIT FINDS PEACE.

LIKE ANGELS' GENTLE GAZE, HER EYES SPARKLED WITH LOVE IN MANY WAYS.

I LOVE THIS LITTLE GIRL. THE WIND SINGS IN RESPONSE AS SHE DANCES WITH BUTTERFLIES ON SILKEN WINGS.

I LOVE THIS LITTLE GIRL. HER SMILE IS SO BRIGHT; IT IS A SUNBEAM'S DELIGHT. IT LIGHTS UP THE DAY AND CHASES AWAY THE NIGHT

WITH JOY IN HER HEART, SHE SPREADS CHEERS TO EVERYONE SHE MEETS.

I LOVE THIS LITTLE GIRL AS HER LAUGHTER ECHOES IN THE WHISPERING WIND,

AND MY HEART GLOWS
AFFECTIONATELY.

I ADORE THIS LITTLE GIRL;
SHE FILLS MY HEART WITH
JOY.

I FEEL A SENSE OF WARMTH AND TENDERNESS I COULD CHERISH FOREVER WHEN I GAZE INTO HER EYES.

I LOVED ONE; I LOVE THEM ALL. LITTLE GIRLS ARE LIKE LITTLE ANGELS.

THEY ARE BRIGHT AND ADD SO MUCH COLOR TO LIFE.

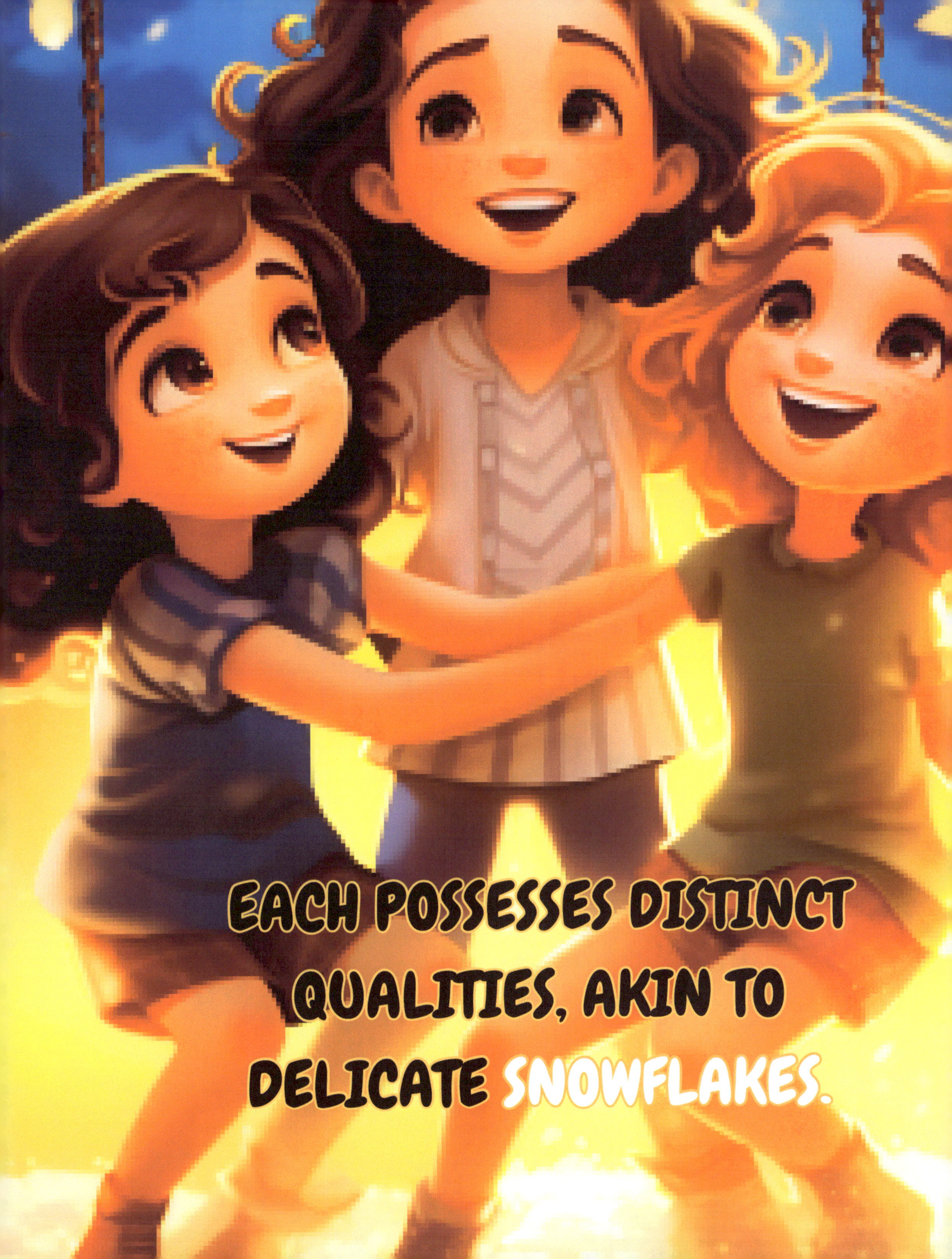

EACH POSSESSES DISTINCT QUALITIES, AKIN TO DELICATE SNOWFLAKES.

AMAZING AND BEAUTIFUL COLORS, EACH FILLED WITH BEAUTIFUL DREAMS. I LOVE THIS LITTLE GIRL

YOU MEAN MUCH MORE THAN WORDS COULD TELL. YOU ARE MY EVERYTHING.

LOVE THIS LITTLE GIRL